J N A N E S H W A R ' S

# HARIPATH

28 ABHANGS IN MARATHI WITH TRANSLITERATION AND ENGLISH AND HINDI TRANSLATIONS

ISBN 978-1-7321420-7-7

Shanti Mandir
51 Muktananda Marg
Walden, NY 12586, U.S.A
+1 (845) 778-1008

The front and back cover pictures are copyrighted by *Santkrupa Pratishthan*, Sadashiv Peth, Pune, and have been supplied for our use by the editor, Bharati Khare. The painting on the front cover was made under the direction of the famous twentieth-century blind Maharashtrian saint Gulābrāo Mahārāj. Gulābrāo Mahārāj used to call himself a daughter of Jñāneśvar. He used his vision of Jñāneśvar to direct the artist. The back cover is a picture of Jñāneśvar's samādhi at Alandi.

Book design: Ron Carter

www.shantimandir.com

*One who stands at*
*God's door even*
*for a moment*
*has attained*
*the four-fold*
*liberation.*

*Haripāṭha, abhang 1*

# PREFACE

JÑĀNEŚVAR (1275-1297) is a favorite saint of Maharashtra, India. He is lovingly called "mother" by devotees. Jñāneśvar's short life falls into two parts. The first ends with his departure from Paithan, a place in Maharashtra famous at the time for learning and wisdom, and includes mainly the persecution that he and his brothers, Nivṛtti and Sopān, and a sister, Muktābāī, were subjected to by the orthodox brahmins of Alandi, his native place. The second comprises the performance of miracles at Paithan, writing of *Jñāneśvarī* and other works at Nevase and other works, his fame and honor all over India, and his entering mahāsamādhi.

Jnāñeśvar brazenly blazed a trail of wisdom and devotion amongst his Maharashtrian brethren that ignited what has been called the "bhakti revolution." He brought the message of unity and oneness of the *Bhagavad Gītā* into Marathi from Sanskrit. This work, titled *Jñāneśvarī*, contains a rich embellishment of colorful, often humorous, similies that entertain and amaze. Jnānadev, another affectionate name given to him, left many other gifts for those seeking a practical, easy, earthy, and enjoyable approach to spirituality.

His work *Amṛtanubhav*, or *Anubhavamṛt*, the "nectar of experience," contains his exposition of the oneness of Śiva and Śakti, the greatness of the Guru, the state that transcends words and speech, the meaning of sat-cit-ānanda, the refutation of knowledge as well as ignorance, and the state of being liberated while alive (jīvanmukta) based on his firsthand experience.

*Caṅgdev Pāsaśṭhī* is his sixty-five-verse response to the 1400-year-old yoga adept Caṅgdev, who sent a blank letter to Jñāneśvar and his siblings, not knowing how to address them so young in age, yet so complete in spiritual knowledge. Jñānadev deftly and sublimely welcomes Caṅgdev, while stating that their meeting will occur without the existence of otherness, because such a duality is truly unreal. In this short work on Reality, he describes how Reality, Consciousness, or Śiva manifests as the entire universe and how the triad of seer, seeing, and seen is created from one and the same Consciousness. As a result, there is no duality whatsoever.

Jñāneśvar also wrote over a thousand abhaṅgs, or unbreakable devotional poems.

**Haripāṭha**: Twenty-eight of his abhaṅgs were written as a collection called *Haripāṭha* (meaning "Sing Hari, study Hari [God]"). Jñāneśvar, his siblings, and many others started on the journey from Alandi to Paithan. Their goal was to obtain the śuddhi patra ("purification document") from the Paithan pandits. Each day, Jñāneśvar wrote an abhaṅg about the importance of singing Hari's name. Walking to reach Paithan took twenty-eight days. After reaching Paithan, Jñāneśvar made a buffalo sing the *Vedas*. Everyone, including the Paithan pandits, was amazed and the pandits gave a śuddhi patra, which was recently published in the Marathi magazine *Santkrupa*. The *Haripāṭha* has been popular in Maharashtra for seven centuries, and its daily recitation is considered a complete spiritual practice. Most of the poems consist of four lines; they have a theme and are punctuated with the signature line "*jñānadev mhaṇe*," meaning "Jñānadev says." Each abhaṅg has its own character and unique flavor. Their messages are simple, direct, sublime, and even implosive. The most subtle, lofty teachings of the *Upaniṣads*, *Bhagavad Gītā*, and *Bhakti Sūtras* are offered to us freely—as Jnanadev says, "like fruit in the palm of our hand."

Jñānadev first tells us that liberation is not as far off and unattainable as we may think. He says, "One who stands at God's door even for a moment has attained the four-fold liberation" (abhaṅg 1). Then he says,

"Hari, the individual soul, and indeed Lord Śiva, are one and the same. Don't weary your mind with difficult paths. For Jñānadev, chanting Hari is heaven itself. You will see this world densely pervaded by Hari" (abhaṅg 2). He extols devotion as the most essential quality in spiritual life, and in abhaṅg 3, he explains, "O how quickly the deity is pleased. Remain quiet in solitude, don't strive needlessly. With such great effort you pursue your worldly life. But why are you not worshipping Hari? Jñānadev says repetition of the name of God will break the world's hold on you" (abhaṅg 3). Perhaps, most importantly, he sings to us about the importance and the impact of the company of the saints. He says, "Whoever attains the understanding of the saints loses his separateness. It dissolves in the experience of the Self. Just as when lighted camphor flames away and ends then and there, leaving no trace, one flourishes in fortune in the territory of liberation when he becomes God's devotee in the company of the saints" (abhaṅg 6). In every verse, like a loving mother, he encourages us to take up the repetition of God's name and hold God close to us. He says, "As one repeats the name of God, millions of sins drop away. Hold onto the thought of Rāma Kṛṣṇa. Extricate all your negative tendencies, cut off all attachments. Don't hide behind the senses. Have faith in the holy places and rituals and always cultivate tenderness, peace, and compassion. In this way, you will make Hari your guest" (abhaṅg 27).

Many of us were fortunate to have sat in the presence of Muktānanda Baba, Swami Muktānanda, who night after night in his spiritual discourses would lovingly refer to the great poet-saints of Maharashtra. He told us the stories of Tukārām, Jñāneśvar, Eknāth, and Nāmdev and sang their abhaṅgs with great joy and love. Through his nectarian words, he granted us access to their time, their devotion, and their eternal wisdom. We are immensely grateful to his successor, Mahāmandaleśvara Gurudev Nityānanda, for emphasizing the chanting of Jñānadev's *Haripāṭha*. We feel ourselves being swept away by the same joy that Baba shared with us. As we sing these beautiful abhaṅgs, and muse over their sublime messages, we may easily experience the truth of Jñānadev's words, "*jñānadevā nāma rāmakṛṣṇī ṭhasā, teṇeṅ daśa-diśā ātmārāma*," "Jñānadev has been stamped with the name Rāma Kṛṣṇa, and now he roams in the bliss of the Self in all ten directions." (abhaṅg 16) Singing the *Haripāṭha* with Gurudev, we are indeed sitting together in Pandharpur with Lord Viṭṭhala and Rukmiṇī. Tukārām, Nāmdev, Eknāth, Sopān, Muktābāī, and Jñānadev himself are swaying, dancing, clapping their hands, laughing, crying, and congratulating us for stepping through the veil of the mind into the boundless world of singing the names of God, in the company of the saints. After perhaps only one such ecstatic session, we are likely to walk away swaying and smiling, as we continue to hear Jñānadev's wonderfully haunting refrain, "*hari mukheṅ mhaṇā, harī mukheṅ mhaṇā, puṇyācī gaṇanā koṇa karī*"–"Chant Hari, chant Hari, who can count the merit to be gained?"

The last abhaṅg in this booklet, which is written as the finale for the recitation, is a prayer by Tukārām extolling the greatness of company of saints of saints, and is sung as the final *Haripāṭha* song by some varkaris (pilgrims) in Maharashtra.

The English translation has been made as literal as possible by Umesh and Chitra Nagarkatte, and was edited by Dana Wilkinson. The Hindi translation was jointly composed by Umesh Nagarkatte and Ashok Vyas. They are all grateful to Jñāneśvar for bestowing bliss on them as they worked on the translation.

Umesh Nagarkatte and Dana Wilkinson

## Guide to Marathi Pronunciation

The dash (-) means "as in the pronunciation of the highlighted letter in the word."

### Vowels

| | | |
|---|---|---|
| **a** – **A**merica | **u** – f**u**ll | **ṛ** - me**rri**ly |
| **ā** – in f**a**ther | **ū** – r**oo**f | **o** – c**o**ne |
| **i** – f**i**sh, w**i**sh | **e** – p**e**tal | **au** – pr**ou**d |
| **ī** – pol**i**ce | **ai** – **ai**sle | **(a)ṁ** – ju**mp** |

### Consonants

***Gutturals*** *(pronounced from throat)*

| | | |
|---|---|---|
| **k** – **c**up | **g** – **g**ive | **ṅ** – si**ng** |
| **kh** – Ec**kh**art | **gh** – di**g-h**ard | |

***Palatals*** *(pronounced with middle of tongue against palate)*

| | | |
|---|---|---|
| **c** – whi**ch** | **j** – **j**oy | **ñ** – ca**ny**on |
| **ch** – staun**ch-h**eart | **jh** – hed**ge-h**og | |

*In Marathi sometimes these letters are aspirated, (i.e., jh pronounced as z), tongue touching teeth, and the places where this occurs are underlined in the booklet to keep the pronunciation genuine. This is an important difference between Marathi and Hindi or Sanskrit, and distinguishes a Marathi speaker from a non-Marathi speaker. In Hindustani – Urdu mixed Hindi, a dot (nuktā) is used below the letter to show this pronunciation. In Marathi there is no nuktā.*

***Cerebrals*** *(pronounced with tip of tongue against roof of mouth)*

| | | |
|---|---|---|
| **ṭ** – **t**ub | **ḍ** – **d**ove | **ṇ** – do**n**'t |
| **ṭh** – ligh**t-h**eart | **ḍh** – re**d-h**ot | |

***Dentals*** *(pronounced as cerebrals but with tongue against teeth)*

| | | |
|---|---|---|
| **t** – wi**t**h | **d** – **th**en | **n** – **n**ut |
| **th** – **th**umb | **dh** – brea**the-h**ere | |

***Labials*** *(pronounced with the lips)*

| | | |
|---|---|---|
| **p** – **p**ine | **b** – **b**ird | **m** – **m**other |
| **ph** – **up-h**ill (not f) | **bh** – ru**b-h**ard | |

| ***Sibilants*** | ***Semivowels*** |
|---|---|
| **ś** – di**sh** | **y** – **y**es |
| **ṣ** – **sh**ow | **r** – **r**un |
| **s** – **s**un | **l** – **l**ight |
| | **v** – **v**ine |

# HARIPATH

## श्री गुरुदेव

**जय जय रामकृष्ण हरी ।**

*jay jay rāmakṛṣṇa harī |*

Hail hail to Rāma, Kṛṣṇa, and Hari.

रूप पाहतां लोचनी सुख[1] झाले वो साजणी ॥१॥
तो हा विठ्ठल बरवा, तो हा माधव बरवा ॥२॥
बहुत सुकृतांची जोडी, म्हणुनि विठ्ठली आवडी ॥३॥
सर्व सुखाचे आगर, बाप रखुमादेवीवर ॥४॥

*rūpa pāhatāṅ locanī sukha jhāle vo sājaṇī.*
*to hā viṭṭhala baravā, to hā mādhava baravā.*
*bahuta sukṛtāṅcī joḍī, mhaṇuni viṭṭhalī āvaḍī.*
*sarva sukhāce āgara, bāpa rakhumādevivara.*

My eyes have seen that form, O dear, I have experienced such joy.
That is this good Viṭṭhala, that is this good Mādhava.
Through great merit I have attained love for Viṭṭhala.
You are the reservoir of all happiness, O father, husband of Rukmiṇī.[2]

रूप देखते आंखोंसे ही, सुख हुआ वो सजनी ॥१॥
ये विठ्ठल ही मन भाया, ये माधव ही सुहाया ॥२॥
बहुत पुण्यों का है ये योग, हुआ है विठ्ठल से संयोग ॥३॥
सब सुखों का आगार, पिता रखुमादेवी[3] का भर्तार ॥४॥

---

[1] नीचे मारी हुई लकीर _ नुक्ता है। मराठी में नुक्ता नही लिखा जाता लेकिन कही जगह उच्चार नुक्ता के साथ करते हैं। The underline indicates the jh has to be pronounced like z in pizza.

[2] Jñānadev's signature. Poets would identify their poetry with specific names, which is their signature.

[3] ज्ञानेश्वर महाराज की निशानी.

# हरिपाठ
## Haripāṭha

1

देवाचिये द्वारी उभा क्षणभरी । तेणें मुक्ति चारी साधीयेल्या ॥१॥
हरि मुखें म्हणा हरि मुखें म्हणा । पुण्याची गणना कोण करी ॥२॥
असोनि संसारीं जिव्हें वेगु करी । वेदशास्त्र उभारी बाह्या सदा ॥३॥
ज्ञानदेव म्हणे व्यासाचिया खुणा । द्वारकेचा राणा पांडवां घरी ॥४॥

*devāciye dvārī ubhā kṣaṇabharī, teṇeṅ mukti cārī sādhīyelyā.*
*hari mukheṅ mhaṇā harī mukheṅ mhaṇā, puṇyācī gaṇanā koṇa karī.*
*asoni saṁsārīṅ jivheṅ vegu karī, veda-śāstra ubhārī bāhyā sadā.*
*jñānadeva mhaṇe vyāsāciyā khuṇā, dvārakecā rāṇā pāṅḍavāṅ* gharī.

One who stands at God's door even for a moment
has attained the four-fold[4] liberation.
Chant "Hari," chant "Hari," who can count the merit to be gained?
Staying in the world, hasten the tongue to repeat the Name,
the Vedas and śāstras declare this arms upraised.
Jñānadev says, "Sage Vyāsa points out that the Pāṇḍavas repeating
the Name brought the king of Dvārakā to their house."

जो ठहरा क्षण भर ठाकुर के द्वार, उस ने साध लीं मुक्तियाँ चार ॥१॥
बोलो हरि मुख से बोलो हरि मुख से, पुण्यों को गिना जाये भी किसी से ॥२॥
संसार में रह कर जिव्हा को चलाये, कहे वेदशास्त्र सदा बाहों को उठाये ॥३॥
ज्ञानदेव कहे व्यासजी बताये, द्वारका का राणा पांडवों के घर आये ॥४॥

हर अभंग के बाद टेक – हरि मुखें म्हणा हरि मुखें म्हणा। पुण्याची गणना कोण करी ॥

Refrain after each song:
*hari mukheṅ mhaṇā, harī mukheṅ mhaṇā, puṇyācī gaṇanā koṇa karī.*
(x 2)

[4] Four-fold refers to samīpatā (closeness with the Lord), sāyujyatā (oneness with the Lord), salokyatā (dwelling in the same place with the Lord), and sarūpatā (being of the same nature as the Lord).

2

चहूं वेदीं जाण साही शास्त्रीं कारण । अठराहि पुराणें हरिसी गाती ॥१॥
मंथुनी नवनीता तैसें घे अनंता । वायां व्यर्थ कथा सांडी मार्ग ॥२॥
एक हरि आत्मा जीवशिव सम । वायां तू दुर्गमां न घाली मन ॥३॥
ज्ञानदेवा पाठ हरि हा वैकुंठ । भरला घनदाट हरि दिसे ॥४॥

*cahūṅ vediṅ jāṇa sāhī śāstrīṅ kāraṇa, aṭharāhi purāṇeṅ harisī gātī.*
*maṅthunī navanītā taiseṅ ghe anaṅtā, vāyāṅ vyartha kathā sāṅḍī mārga.*
*eka hari ātmā jīvaśiva sama, vāyāṅ tū durgamāṅ na ghālī mana.*
*jñānadevā pāṭha hari hā vaikuṇṭha, bharalā ghana-dāṭa hari dise.*

Know that the goal of all four *Vedas* and six śāstras and
eighteen *Purāṇas*[5] is to sing praises of Hari.
Churning these (and also churning the world), the cream
you get is the Supreme.
Give up all other futile paths as gossip.
Hari and the individual Self are one; jīva (individual) and Śiva (God)
are one. Don't weary your mind with difficult paths.
For Jñānadev, chanting Hari is heaven itself.
You see the world densely pervaded by Hari.

चार वेदों, छः शास्त्रों का कारण ले जान, अठारह पुराण भी करे हरि का ही गान ॥१॥
मथ के मक्खन वैसा अनंत ले लो, और मार्ग जो हैं व्यर्थ गप, छोड दो ॥२॥
एक हरि और आत्मा जीव हैं शिव सम, मत डाल मन मार्ग में दुर्गम ॥३॥
हरिपाठ ही वैकुंठ ज्ञानदेव का, भरा सघन हरि हरि दिखता ॥४॥

---

[5] The four *Vedas* are *Ṛgveda, Yajurveda, Sāmaveda*, and *Atharvaveda*. The *Upaniṣads* are parts of the *Vedas*. The six śāstras (philosophies) are Nyāya (jurisprudence) of Sage Gautama, Vaisheṣika of Sage Kaṇād, Sānkhya of Sage Kapila, Yoga of Sage Patañjali, Pūrva Mīmāṁsā (thought emphasizing action) of Sage Jaimini, Uttar Mimāṁsā (emphasizing knowledge) from the *Upaniṣads*. "*Brahma satyam jaganmithyā, jivo brahmaiva nāparaḥ*" ("Brahman is the Truth, the world is illusory. An individual is Brahman Itself and no other.") is the doctrine of the *Upaniṣads*. The eighteen *Purāṇas* are epics that describe tradition and discuss dharma (righteousness); compiled by Sage Vyāsa, they are *Brahma, Padma, Viṣṇu, Vāyu, Bhāgavat, Bhaviṣya, Nārada, Mārkaṇḍeya, Agni, Brahma-vaivarta, Liṅga, Varāha, Skanda, Vāmana, Kūrma, Matsya, Garuḍa, Brahmāṇḍa*. The *Purāṇas* consist of 400,000 verses (based on explanations by Dhuṇḍā Mahārāj Degalūrkar in *Haripāṭha Vivaraṇa*).

3

त्रिगुण असार निर्गुण हें सार । सारासार विचार हरिपाठ ॥१॥
सगुण निर्गुण गुणाचें अगुण । हरिवीण मन व्यर्थ जाय ॥२॥
अव्यक्त निराकार नाही त्या आकार । जेथोनि चराचर हरिसी भजे ॥३॥
ज्ञानदेवा ध्यानीं रामकृष्ण मनीं । अनंत जन्मोनी पुण्य होय ॥४॥

*triguṇa asāra nirguṇa he sāra, sārāsāra vicāra haripāṭha.*
*saguṇa nirguṇa guṇāceṅ aguṇa, harivīṇa mana vyartha jāya.*
*avyakta nirākāra nāhī tyā ākāra, jethoni carācara harisī bhaje.*
*jñānadevā dhyānīṅ rāma-rṛṣṇa manīṅ, anaṅta janmonī puṇya hoya.*

What is composed of the three guṇas (qualities) is unreal, and what is without guṇas is the real. Repeating "Hari" is discriminating between the real and unreal.
Mind thinking about form and formlessness is wasted, if it is not thinking of Hari, who is beyond both.
Worship Hari, who is without manifestation or form and has no shape, but from whom the sentient and insentient universe arises.
Jñānadev's mind meditates on Rāma Kṛṣṇa; that is the result of merits of countless lifetimes.

त्रिगुन असार निर्गुन है सार, हरिपाठ है सारासार विचार ॥१॥
सगुन या निर्गुन गुनों के परे अगुन, बिना हरि के व्यर्थ हो जाता है मन ॥२॥
अव्यक्त और निराकार ना उसे आकार, उस हरि को भजो जहाँ से निकले चराचर ॥३॥
ज्ञानदेव ध्यान राम कृष्ण मन में, पुण्य जागे, किये अनंत जनम में ॥४॥

4

भावेंविण भक्ति, भक्तिवीण मुक्ति । बळेवीण शक्ति, बोलूं नये ॥१॥
कैसेनि दैवत प्रसन्न त्वरीत । उगा राहे निवांत शिणसी वायां ॥२॥
सायास करिसी प्रपंच दिननिशीं । हरिसी न भजसी कवण्या गुणे ॥३॥
ज्ञानदेव म्हणे हरिजप करणें । तुटेल धरणे प्रपंचाचे ॥४॥

*bhāveviṇa bhakti, bhakti viṇa mukti, baḷeviṇa śakti, boluṅ naye.*
*kaiseni daivata prasanna tvarīta, ugā rāhe nivāṅta śiṇasī vāyāṅ.*
*sāyāsa karisī prapaṅca dina-niśīṅ, harīsī na bhajasī kavaṇyā guṇe.*
*jñānadeva mhaṇe harijapa karaṇeṅ, tuṭela dharaṇe prapaṅcāce.*

Bhakti without feeling, liberation without bhakti (devotion),
power (śakti) without strength should not be talked about.
O how quickly the diety is pleased. Remain quiet in solitude,
you strive needlessly.
With great effort, you are preoccupied with worldly life.
Why are you not worshipping Hari?
Jñānadev says, "Doing Hari japa (mantra repetition)
breaks the world's hold on you."

भाव बिना भक्ति, भक्ति बिना मुक्ति, बोलो मत बल की बात बिना शक्ति ॥१॥
दैवत कैसे प्रसन्न त्वरित, बैठे आराम एकांत में, प्रयास करे व्यर्थ ॥२॥
प्रपंच दिनरात आयास करे, काहे के लिये हरि का भजन ना करे ॥३॥
ज्ञानदेव कहे हरिजप करना, टूट जाये प्रपंच का पकड़ना ॥४॥

5

योगयागविधि येणें नोहे सिद्धि । वायांचि उपाधि दंभधर्म ॥१॥
भावेविण देव न कळे निःसंदेह । गुरुविणे अनुभव कैसा कळे ॥२॥
तपेविण दैवत दिधल्याविण प्राप्त । गुजेविण हित कोण सांगे ॥३॥
ज्ञानदेव सांगे दृष्टांताची मात । साधुचे संगतीं तरणोपाय ॥४॥

*yoga-yāga-vidhi yeṇeṅ nohe siddhi, vāyāṅci upādhi daṁbha dharma.*
*bhāveviṇa deva na kaḷe nis-saṅdeha, guruviṇe anubhava kaisā kaḷe.*
*tapeviṇa daivata didhalyāviṇa prāpta, gujeviṇa hita koṇa sāṅge.*
*jñānadeva sāṅge dṛṣṭaṅtācī māta sādhuce saṅgatīṅ taraṇopāya.*

Yoga, yagña (fire ritual), and rituals will not bring realization.
All this striving brings false praise.
Without devotion, it is certain that you will not understand God.
How will you get experience without the Guru?
Just as God is not pleased unless you perform practices and
make offerings, if you do not reveal your heart's secret (love),
how can the Guru bestow his grace on you?
Jñānadev describes what he has seen, remaining in the company
of the saints is the means to go across.

योगयागविधि इससे नहीं सिद्धि, दांभिक धर्म की व्यर्थ उपाधि ।।१।।
भावबिना देव न समझे निःसंदेह, कैसे आवे गुरु बिना अनुभव ।।२।।
तप किये बिना देव संग कैसे हो ले, गूढ प्रेम बिना हित कौन बोले ।।३।।
ज्ञानदेव बोले अनुभव की बात, है तरने के उपाय साधू के साथ ।।४।।

6

साधुबोध झाला तो नुरोनिया ठेला । ठायींच मुराला अनुभव ॥१॥
कापुराची वाती उजळली ज्योती । ठायींच समाप्ती झाली जैशी ॥२॥
मोक्ष रेखे आला भाग्यें विनटला । साधूंचा अंकिला हरिभक्त ॥३॥
ज्ञानदेवा गोडी संगती सज्जनीं । हरि दिसे जनींवनीं आत्मतत्त्वीं ॥४॥

*sādhubodha jhālā to nuroniyā ṭhelā, ṭhāyiṅca murālā anubhava.*
*kāpurāci vātī ujaḷalī jyotī, ṭhāyiṅca samāptī jhālī jaiśī.*
*mokṣa rekhe ālā bhāgyeṅ vinaṭalā, sādhūṅcā ankilā hari-bhakta.*
*jñānadevā goḍī saṅgatī sajjanīṅ, hari dise janīṅ-vanīṅ ātma-tattvīṅ.*

Whoever attains the understanding of the saints loses his separateness.
It dissolves in the experience of the Self,
just as the lighted camphor flames away and ends then and there,
leaving no trace.
One flourishes in fortune in the territory of liberation,
when a devotee of God has been touched by saints.
Jñānadev experiences nectar in the company of saints,
and sees Hari in people, the forest, and Self.

साधु का बोध आया, अलगपना गँवाया, वो तो घुलमिल पाया ॥
कपूर की बत्ती की उजली ज्योति, उसी जगह जैसे समाप्त होती ॥
मोक्ष देहरी आया, भाग्य इठलाया, हरिभक्त पर साधू ने मुहर लगाया ॥
ज्ञानदेव को सत्संगत में मिला अमृत, जन वन और आत्मतत्त्व में हरि है निहारत ॥

## 7

पर्वताप्रमाणे पातक करणें । वज्रलेप होणें अभक्तासी ॥१॥
नाहीं ज्यासी भक्ति ते पतीत अभक्त । हरिसी न भजत दैवहत ॥२॥
अनंत वाचाळ बरळती बरळ । त्या कैंचा दयाळ पावे हरि ॥३॥
ज्ञानदेवा प्रमाण आत्मा हा निधान । सर्वांघटीं पूर्ण एक नांदे ॥४॥

*parvatā-pramāṇe pātaka karaṇeṅ, vajralepa hoṇeṅ abhaktāsī.*
*nāhīṅ jyāsī bhakti te patīta abhakta, harisī na bhajata daivahata.*
*anaṅta vācāḷa baraḷatī baraḷa, tyā kaiṅcā dayāḷa pāve hari.*
*jñānadevā pramāṇa ātmā hā nidhāna, sarvāṅghaṭīṅ pūrṇa eka nāṅde.*

Creating a mountain of sins forms a diamond-hard crust
around the non-devotee.
They who have no love for God are downtrodden agnostics,
destroyed by destiny, without remembrance of Hari.
How can compassionate Hari bestow His grace upon
those who babble endless gossip?
Jñānadev testifies that the Self is the refuge
that alone blissfully permeates all forms.

पर्वत जितने पाप घट जाये, अभक्त से वो वज्र ज्यूं लिपट जाये॥
नहीं जिन्हें भक्ति वे पतित अभक्त, हरि को न भजते अभाग से आहत ॥
गपिया अनंत गपशप तुतलाये, उन्हें वह दयालु हरि कैसे पाये ॥
ज्ञानदेव की साक्ष्य आत्मा ही लक्ष्य, सब घट में एकरस पूर्ण है प्रत्यक्ष ॥

8

संतांचे संगति मनोमार्ग गति । आकळावा श्रीपति येणे पंथे ॥१॥
रामकृष्ण वाचा भाव हा जिवाचा । आत्मा जो शिवाचा रामजप ॥२॥
एकतत्त्व नाम साधिती साधन । द्वैताचे बंधन न बाधिजे ॥३॥
नामामृत गोडी वैष्णवां लाधली । योगियां साधली जीवनकळा ॥४॥
सत्वर उच्चार प्रल्हादीं बिंबला । उद्धवा लाधला कृष्णदाता ॥५॥
ज्ञानदेव म्हणे नाम हें सुलभ । सर्वत्र दुर्लभ विरळा जाणे ॥६॥

*saṅtāṅce saṅgati manomārga gati, ākaḷāvā śripati yeṇe paṅthe.*
*rama-kṛṣṇa vācā bhāva ha jivācā, ātmā jo śivācā rāmajapa.*
*eka-tattva nāma sādhitī sādhana, dvaitāce baṅdhana na bādhije.*
*nāmāmṛta goḍī vaiṣṇavāṅ lādhalī, yogiyāṅ sādhalī jīvanakaḷā.*
*satvara uccāra prahlādīṅ bimbalā, uddhavā lādhalā kṛṣṇa-dātā.*
*jñānadev mhaṇe nāma heṅ sulabha, sarvatra durlabha viraḷā jāṇe.*

The company of saints directs our mind to the right path
through which we should attain the Lord.
To repeat "Rāma Kṛṣna" is the nature of the individual,
Lord Śiva's soul is the japa of Rāma.
Repeating the Name is the only practice to attain the One Principle.
The fetters of duality do not affect those who attain it.
Devotees of the Lord are rejuvenated by the sweetness of the nectar
of the Name, just as yogis are with nectar from the cranium.
When they repeated His Name, the Lord appeared instantly before
Prahlād and Uddhava met his benefactor, Kṛṣṇa.
Jñānadev says, "Though simple, all find this Name difficult;
only a rare one knows about this."

संतों की संगति से मन की मार्गपर गति, यही रास्ते से प्राप्त होते हैं श्रीपति ॥
वाचा से राम कृष्ण, है भाव जीव का, रामजप ही है आत्मा शिव का ॥
एक तत्त्व नाम से साधित होता है, द्वैत का बंधन न बाधित होता है ॥
नामामृत की मिठाई, वैष्णवों को खिलाई, योगियों को जीवन की सुधा पिलाई ॥
त्वरित उच्चार से प्रह्लाद लाभ उठाया, उद्धव को दाता कृष्ण मिल पाया ॥
ज्ञानदेव कहे नाम यह सुलभ, विरला ही जाने, सभी को लगे दुर्लभ ॥

9

विष्णुविणें जप व्यर्थ त्याचें ज्ञान । रामकृष्णीं मन नाहीं ज्याचें ॥१॥
उपजोनि करंटा नेणें अद्वैत वाटा । रामकृष्णीं पैठा कैसा होय ॥२॥
द्वैताची झाडणी गुरुवीण ज्ञान । त्या कैचें कीर्तन घडेल नामीं ॥३॥
ज्ञानदेव म्हणे सगुण हें ध्यान । नामपाठ मौन प्रपंचाचे ॥४॥

*viṣṇuviṇeṅ japa vyartha tyāceṅ jñāna, rāma-kṛṣṇīṅ mana nāhīṅ jyāceṅ.*
*upajoni karaṅṭā neṇeṅ advaita vāṭā, rāma-kṛṣṇīṅ paiṭhā kaisā hoya.*
*dvaitācī jhāḍaṇī guru-vīṇa jñāna, tyā kaiceṅ kīrtana ghaḍel nāmīṅ.*
*jñānadeva mhaṇe saguṇa heṅ dhyāna, nāmapāṭha mouna prapaṅcāce.*

Except for Viṣṇu's japa, any other japa is futile. That person's
knowledge is futile, whose mind is not established in Rāma Kṛṣṇa.
Unfortunate indeed is he who, having taken birth, does not know
the path of nonduality. How can he take refuge in Rāma Kṛṣṇa?
Knowledge from the Guru alone can get rid of duality.
How can one have devotion for the Name if duality is not eradicated?
Jñānadev says, "Repeating the Name is meditation on the
form of the Lord and silences the world."

विष्णु बिना जप व्यर्थ उस का ज्ञान, राम कृष्ण नाम में नही जिस का मन ॥
पैदा हो के दरिद्र न जाने अद्वैत की राह, राम कृष्ण में उस की बढे कैसे चाह॥
कैसे द्वैत का झाड़न, ज्ञान गुरुबिना, कैसे नाम का कीर्तन होये गुरुबिना ॥
ज्ञानदेव कहे सगुण यह ध्यान, नामपाठ प्रपंच को कर देता है मौन ॥

**जय जय विठोबा रखुमाई...**

*jay jay viṭhobā rakhumāi...*

Hail hail to Viṭhobā Rakhumāi ...

10

**त्रिवेणी संगमीं नाना तीर्थें भ्रमी । चित्त नाही नामीं तरी तें व्यर्थ ॥१॥**
**नामासी विन्मुख तो नर पापिया । हरिवीण धांवया न पवे कोणी ॥२॥**
**पुराणप्रसिद्ध बोलिले वाल्मिक । नामें तिन्ही लोक उद्धरती ॥३॥**
**ज्ञानदेव म्हणे नाम जपा हरीचे । परंपरा त्याचें कुळ शुद्ध ॥४॥**

*triveṇī saṅgamīṅ nānā tīrtheṅ bhramī, citta nāhīṅ nāmīṅ tarī teṅ vyartha.*
*nāmāsī vinmukha to nara pāpiyā, harīvīṇa dhāṅvayā na pave koṇī.*
*purāṇa-prasiddha bolile vālmika, nāmeṅ tinhī loka uddharatī.*
*jñānadeva mhaṇe nāma japā harīce, paraṁparā tyāceṅ kuḷa śuddha.*

Pilgrimages to the confluence of three rivers and other holy places
are in vain if the mind is not established in the Name.
That person is a sinner who has turned away from the Name.
There is no one else except Hari who can protect one from sins.
Sages, such as Vālmīki, who are well-known from the *Purāṇas*
have said that the Name redeems all the three worlds.
Jñānadev says, "Repeat Hari's name. Then all your family
and lineage will be purified."

त्रिवेणी संगम जाये है, कयी तीर्थस्थान हो आये, चित्त नाम में बिना, व्यर्थ सब हो जाये ॥
नाम से विमुख पापी है नर, हरि बिना दौड़ कौन ले खबर॥
पुराण के प्रसिद्ध बोले वे वाल्मिकी, नाम से पार होते हैं त्रिलोकी ॥
ज्ञानदेव कहे नाम जपे हरि का, परंपरा कुल शुध्द होवे उसी का ॥

11

हरि उच्चारणीं अनंत पापराशी । जातील लयासी क्षणमात्रे ॥१॥
तृण अग्निमेळे समरस झाले । तैसे नामें केलें जपतां हरि ॥२॥
हरि उच्चारण मंत्र पैं अगाध । पळे भूतबाधा भेणें तेथें ॥३॥
ज्ञानदेव म्हणे हरि माझा समर्थ । न करवे अर्थ उपनिषदां ॥४॥

*harī uccāraṇīṁ ananta pāparāśī, jātīla layāsī kṣaṇamātre.*
*tṛṇa agnimeḷe samarasa jhāle, taise nāmeṁ keleṁ japatāṁ hari.*
*hari uccāraṇa mantra paiṁ agādha, paḷe bhūtabādhā bheṇeṁ tetheṁ.*
*jñānadeva mhaṇe hari mājhā samartha, na karave artha upaniṣadāṁ.*

As you utter the name of Hari, infinite piles of sins
are destroyed in a moment.
When grass touches fire, it burns to ashes; so do sins
burn down when touched by Hari's name.
Therefore the power of Hari mantra is unfathomable,
the affliction of the five elements runs away with fear.
Jñānadev says, "My Hari is all-powerful. Even the *Upaniṣads*
cannot describe His power."

हरि उच्चारण से अनंत पाप का भंडार, क्षण भर में हो जाये उसी का संहार ॥
जैसे आग तिनके को निगल जाये, हरि नाम जपने से पाप जल जाये ॥
हरि उच्चारण ही मंत्र है अगाध, भूत बाधाएँ भय से जाये भाग॥
ज्ञानदेव कहे हरि मेरा इतना है समर्थ, उपनिषद भी बता न पाये उसका अर्थ ॥

12

तीर्थव्रत नेम भावेंवीण सिद्धी । वायांची उपाधी करिसी जनां ॥१॥
भावबळे आकळे येर्हवी नाकळे । करतळीं आवळे तैसा हरि ॥२॥
पारियाचा रवा घेतां भूमीवरी । यत्न परोपरी साधन तैसें ॥३॥
ज्ञानदेव म्हणे निवृत्ति निर्गुण । दिधले संपूर्ण माझे हातीं ॥४॥

*tīrtha-vrata nema bhāveṅ-vīṇa siddhī, vāyāṅcī upādhī karisī janāṅ.*
*bhāva-baḷe ākaḷe yerhavī nākaḷe, karataḷīṅ āvaḷe taisā hari.*
*pāriyācā ravā ghetāṅ bhūmīvarī, yatna paroparī sādhana taiseṅ.*
*jñānadeva mhaṇe nivṛtti nirguṇa, didhale saṁpūrṇa mājhe hatīṅ.*

Any occult powers gained by pilgrimages, austerities, and
spiritual practices done without intense feeling are
empty achievements to impress people.
With the power of intense feeling alone the Lord is attained,
like a myrobylan (small round fruit) in the palm of a hand,[6]
and not any other way.
Like collecting small granules of mercury from the floor,
other spiritual paths involve numerous efforts.
Jñānadev says, "Guru Nivṛtti, who is beyond any attributes,
has placed the whole knowledge in my hand."

त्तीर्थ-विधि-नियम परे सिद्धि बिना भाव की, उपाधि वह व्यर्थ, जो बस हेतु लोगों पर प्रभाव की ॥
भाव के बल से समझे, और किसी तरह नहीं, हरि मिले हथेली की आंवले की तरह यहीं ॥
जमा करे पारा जमीन पर बिखरा हुआ, वैसे और किसी साधना का प्रयत्न बहुतसा हुआ॥
ज्ञानदेव कहे निवृत्ति[7] निर्गुन, मेरे हाथ दिये निर्गुन संपूर्ण ॥

[6] This is a Marathi saying to describe an effortless achievement.
[7] ज्ञानेश्वर महाराज जी के गुरु का नाम

13

समाधी हरीची समसुखेंवीण । न साधेल जाण द्वैतबुद्धि ॥१॥
बुद्धीचे वैभव अन्य नाहीं दुजें । एका केशवराजें सकळ सिद्धी ॥२॥
ऋद्धि सिद्धि निधि अवघीच उपाधी । जंव त्या परमानंदीं मन नाहीं ॥३॥
ज्ञानदेवीं रम्य रमलें समाधान । हरीचें चिंतन सर्वकाळ ॥४॥

*samādhī harīcī samasukheṅvīṇa, na sādhel jāṇa dvaitabuddhi.*
*buddhice vaibhava anya nāhī dujeṅ, ekā keśava-rajeṅ sakaḷa siddhī.*
*ṛddhi siddhī nidhi avaghīca upādhī,*
*jaṅva tyā paramānaṅdīṅ mana nāhīṅ.*
*jñānadevīṅ ramya ramaleṅ samādhāna, harīce ciṅtana sarvakāḷa.*

Know that the intellect of duality will never attain the bliss of equality,
and without the bliss of equality, Hari's samādhi
(perfect absorption) cannot be attained.
There is no other greatness for the intellect except attaining Viṭṭhala,
which brings all siddhis (powers and achievements).
The wealth of ṛddhis (powers of supremacy) and siddhis
(occult powers) are all hindrances, as long as the mind
is not established in the supreme bliss.
Contentment joyfully dwells in Jñānadev,
as contemplation of Hari goes on at all times.

समता के सुख बिना हरी की समाधि न आये, जानो! द्वैतबुद्धि से समता न सध पाये ॥
कुछ और दूसरा नहीं बुद्धि का वैभव, सारी सिद्धियाँ साधे, है एक केशव॥
रिद्धि, सिद्धि, निधि, सब बनते रुकावट, जब तक परमानंद की मन में नही तरावट ॥
रम्य समाधान ज्ञानदेव में मगन, हर समय चले हरि का सुमिरन ॥

14

नित्य सत्य मित हरिपाठ ज्यासी । कळिकाळ त्यासी न पाहे दृष्टि ॥१॥
रामकृष्ण वाचा अनंत राशी तप । पापाचे कळप पळती पुढे ॥२॥
हरि हरि हरि मंत्र हा शिवाचा । म्हणती जे वाचा तया मोक्ष ॥३॥
ज्ञानदेवा पाठ नारायण नाम । पाविजे उत्तम निजस्थान ॥४॥

*nitya satya mita haripāṭha jyāsī, kaḷikāḷa tyāsī na pāhe dṛṣṭī.*
*rāmakṛṣṇa vācā ananta rāśī tapa, pāpāce kaḷapa paḷatī puḍhe.*
*hari hari hari mantra hā śivācā, mhaṇatī je vācā tayā mokṣa.*
*jñānadevā pāṭha nārayaṇa nāma, pāvije uttama nijasthāna.*

Death does not dare to look at him who recites
Hari constantly, sincerely, or even a little.
Uttering Rāma Kṛṣṇa is worth countless loads of austerities,
runaway throngs of sins.
The mantra of Śiva is "Hari, Hari, Hari."
Whoever utters this is liberated.
Jñānadev's path is repeating the name "Nārāyaṇa,"
attain the supreme destination (Self).

नित्य सत्य मित हरिपाठ है जो करता, कलिकाल उसपर नज़र न धरता ॥
रामकृष्ण वाणी से तपों की अनंत राशि जागे, भीड़ पापों की दौड़ जाये आगे ॥
हरि हरि हरि शिव के यह मंत्र-उक्ति, करते रहे जो वाणी से उन्हें मिले मुक्ति ॥
ज्ञानदेव का पाठ नारायण नाम, पहुँचाये उत्तम निज धाम ॥

15

एक नाम हरि द्वैतनाम दुरी । अद्वैतकुसरी विरळा जाणे ॥१॥
समबुद्धि घेतां समान श्रीहरि । शमदमा वरी हरि झाला ॥२॥
सर्वांघटीं राम देहादेही एक । सूर्यप्रकाशक सहस्ररश्मी ॥३॥
ज्ञानदेवा चित्तीं हरिपाठ नेमा । मागिलिया जन्मा मुक्त झालों ॥४॥

*eka nāma hari dvaita-nāma durī, advaita-kusarī viraḷā jāṇe.*
*sama-buddhi ghetāṅ samāna śrihari, śama-damā varī hari jhālā.*
*sarvāṅ-ghaṭiṅ rāma dehādehī eka, sūrya-prakāśaka sahsara-raśmī.*
*jñānadevā cittī hari-pāṭha nemā, māgiliyā janmā mukta jhāloṅ.*

With the name of Hari alone, any trace of duality disappears.
Rarely anyone knows the secret of nonduality.
With the intellect of equality, the Lord is experienced equally everywhere. Transcending tranquility and self-restraint, one becomes Hari.
One Rāma exists in all different forms,
just as the same sun is in thousands of rays.
Jñānadev says, "My mind is set to *Haripāṭha* (repetition of Hari),
I became free from future births."

एक हरि का नाम, भगाये द्वैत का नामोनिशान, बिरला ही पाये अद्वैत का गूढ ज्ञान।।
समबुद्धि से समरस अपनाते श्री हरि, शमदम पार जा के बन जाते श्री हरि ॥
घट घट में, एक रूप से वही राम सार, एक सूर्य से हुई प्रकाशित जैसे किरन हजार ॥
ज्ञानदेव के मन में हरिपाठ नियम से, मुक्त हुवा आगे आने वाले जनम से ॥

16

हरिनाम जपे तो नर दुर्लभ । वाचेसी सुलभ राम कृष्ण ॥१॥
राम कृष्ण नामीं उन्मनी साधली । तयासी लाधली सकळ सिद्धि ॥२॥
सिद्धि बुद्धि धर्म हरिपाठी आले । प्रपंचीं निमाले साधुसंगें ॥३॥
ज्ञानदेवा नाम रामकृष्णीं ठसा । तेणें दशदिशा आत्माराम ॥४॥

*hari-nāma jape to nara durlabha, vācesī sulabha rāma kṛṣṇa.*
*rāma kṛṣṇa nāmīṅ unmanī sādhalī, tayāsī lādhalī sakaḷa siddhi.*
*siddhi buddhi dharma hari-pāṭhī āle, prapañcīṅ nimāle sādhusaṅgeṅ.*
*jñānadevā nāma rāmakṛṣṇī ṭhasā, teṇeṅ daśa-diśā ātmārāma.*

The one who repeats Hari's name is rare,
even though Rāma Kṛṣṇa is easy to say.
Immersed in the name Rāma Kṛṣṇa, whoever goes beyond
the mind receives everything worth achieving.
In the repetition of Hari, all achievements, all intellect,
all righteous actions are included; in the company of saints,
these are calmed from worldliness.
Jñānadev was imprinted with the Rāma Kṛṣṇa name,
by which he experienced the bliss of the Self in all ten[8] directions.

हरिनाम जपे वह नर है दुर्लभ, यूँ रामकृष्ण जपना सहज ही सुलभ ॥
राम कृष्ण में जिसका लीन हुआ मन, दौड आये सभी सिद्धियाँ उन के आंगन ॥
सिद्धि बुद्धि धर्म हरिपाठ में आये, प्रपंच के झंझट सत्संग से छूट जाये ॥
ज्ञानदेव पर अंकित रामकृष्ण नाम, उस से दसों दिशाएँ हो गयीं आत्माराम ॥

[8] East, south, west, north, northeast, southeast, southwest, northwest, up, down.

17

हरिपाठकीर्ति मुखें जरी गाय । पवित्रचि होय देह त्याचा ॥१॥
तपाचें सामर्थ्यें तपिन्नला अमूप । चिरंजीव कल्प वैकुंठी नांदे ॥२॥
मातृ पितृ भ्राता सगोत्र अपार । चतुर्भुज नर होउनि ठेले ॥३॥
ज्ञान गूढगम्य ज्ञानदेवा लाधलें । निवृत्तिनें दिधलें माझे हातीं ॥४॥

*haripāṭha kīrti mukheṅ jarī gāya, pavitraci hoya deha tyācā.*
*tapāceṅ sāmarthye tapinnalā amūpa, ciraṅjīva kalpa vaikuṇṭhī nāṅde.*
*mātṛu pitṛu bhrātā sagotra apāra, caturbhuja nara houni ṭhele.*
*jñāna gūḍha-gamya jñānadevā lādhaleṅ, nivṛttine didhale mājhe hātīṅ.*

When a person who sings the fame of Hari's name,
his body itself is purified.
By the power of austerity of Hari's name when the body
and mind get immersed, he becomes immortal and enjoys
millions of years in Viṣṇu's abode.
His mother, father, brother, and all relatives become one
with Lord Viṣṇu (receive liberation).
Jñānadev received this secret knowledge,
Nivṛtti bestowed it in my hands.

हरिपाठ महिमा का करता जो गायन, हो जायी देह उस की तो पावन ॥
तप के सामर्थ्य से तपा हुवा अमित, चिरंजीव कल्प वैकुंठ में है रहत ॥
माता पिता बंधु सगेवाले अपार, सभी चतुर्भूज हो गये साकार ॥
ज्ञान गूढ गम्य ज्ञानदेव पाया, निवृत्ति के हाथों वह मेरे हाथ आया ॥

18

हरिवंश पुराण हरिनाम कीर्तन । हरिविणे सौजन्य नेणें कांहीं ॥१॥
त्या नरा लाधलें वैकुंठ जोडलें । सकळ घडलें तीर्थाटण ॥२॥
मनोमार्गे गेला तो तेथें मुकला । हरिपाठीं स्थिरावला तोचि धन्य ॥३॥
ज्ञानदेवा गोडी हरिनामाची जोडी । रामकृष्णीं आवडी सर्वकाळ ॥४॥

*hari-vaṅśa purāṇa hari-nāma kīrtana,*
*hari-viṇe saujanya neṇeṅ kāṅhīṅ.*
*tyā narā lādhaleṅ vaikuṅṭha joḍaleṅ,*
*sakaḷa ghaḍaleṅ tīrthāṭaṇa.*
*manomārgeṅ gelā to tetheṅ mukalā,*
*haripāṭhīṅ sthirāvalā toci dhanya.*
*jñānadevā goḍī harināmācī joḍī, rāmakṛṣṇīṅ āvaḍī sarvakāḷa.*

Whoever reads the *Purānas* of Hari's lineage and sings Hari's name
knows nothing else but Hari's compassion.
He is bestowed Vaikuṇṭha (Hari's abode; i.e., he receives liberation),
achieves everything, and has done all pilgrimages.
Whoever follows the mental tendencies is lost there,
whoever is established in repeating "Hari" is blessed indeed.
Jñānadev says, "Love for Hari's name is my attainment.
I have love for Rāma Kṛṣṇa all the time."

बाचे हरिवंश पुराण, हरिनाम गाई, मानो हरिबिना और न सहाई ॥
वह नर पाया वैकुंठ मिलाया, वह सभी तीर्थयात्राएँ कर आया ॥
मन के पथ पर गया वह वहीं खो गया, हरिपाठ में स्थिर हुवा वह धन्य हो गया ॥
ज्ञानदेव की मधुर हरिनाम ही कमाई, रामकृष्ण से सदा प्रेम की सगाई ॥

जय जय विठोबा रखुमाई ...
*jay jay viṭhobā rakhumāi...*
Hail hail to Viṭhobā Rakhumāi...

19

नामसंकीर्तन वैष्णवांची जोडी । पापें अनंत कोडी गेली त्यांची ॥१॥
अनंत जन्मांचें तप एक नाम । सर्व मार्ग सुगम हरिपाठ ॥२॥
योग याग क्रिया धर्माधर्म माया । गेले ते विलया हरिपाठीं ॥३॥
ज्ञानदेवीं यज्ञयाग क्रिया धर्म । हरिवीण नेम नाहीं दूजा ॥४॥

*nāmasaṅkīrtana vaiṣṇavāñcī joḍī, pāpeṅ anaṅta koḍī gelī tyāñcī.*
*anaṅta janmāñceṅ tapa eka nāma, sarva mārga sugama haripāṭha.*
*yoga yāga kriyā dharmā-dharma māyā, gele te vilayā haripāṭhīṅ.*
*jñānadevīṅ yajña-yāga kriyā dharma, harivīṇa nema nāhīṅ dūjā.*

The devotees of Viṣṇu achieve the continuous repetition of the Name
by which their countless millions of sins drop away.
Penances of countless lives are equal to one Name in merit;
repeating the name of Hari is the easiest of all spiritual paths.
Yogas, sacrifices, rituals, righteous or unrighteous tendencies,
and illusion get dissolved in the *Haripāṭha*.
For Jñānadev, Hari is all yajñas, sacrifices, rituals, and
righteous actions. There is no practice other than Hari.

वैष्णवों संग जुडा नामसंकीर्तन, अनंत कोटी पापों का हुआ शमन ॥
एक नाम अनंत जन्मों के तप समान, हर मार्ग से सुगम हरिपाठ प्रस्थान ॥
योग यज्ञ क्रिया और धर्म अधर्म की माया, विलीन हरिपाठ में सब हो पाया ॥
ज्ञानदेव कहें यज्ञ याग क्रिया धरम, हरि बिना नहीं दूसरा कोई नियम ॥

20

वेदशास्त्रपुराण श्रुतींचें वचन । एक नारायण सार जप ॥१॥
जप तप कर्म हरिवीण धर्म । वाउगाचि श्रम व्यर्थ जाय ॥२॥
हरिपाठीं गेले ते निवांतचि ठेले । भ्रमर गुंतले सुमनकळिके ॥३॥
ज्ञानदेवा मंत्र हरिनामाचे शस्त्र । यमें कुळगोत्र वर्जियेलें ॥४॥

*veda-śāstra-purāṇa śrutīnceṅ vacana, eka nārāyaṇa sāra japa.*
*japa tapa karma harivīṇa dharma, vāugāci śrama vyartha jāya.*
*haripāṭhīṅ gele te nivāṅtaci ṭhele, bhramara guṅtale sumana-kaḷike.*
*ññānadevā mantra hari-nāmāce śastra, yameṅ kuḷagotra varjīyeleṅ.*

The *Vedas*, *śāstras*, *Purāṇas*, and *Upaniṣads* promise that repeating
one name, Nārāyaṇa, is the essence of all spiritual practices.
Japa, penances, rituals, and righteous actions without (the thought of)
Hari are unnecessary exertions that go to waste.
Those who go on repeating "Hari" remain at peace.
They are like the bees absorbed in enjoying honey in the flower buds.
For Jñānadev, the mantra of Hari's name is a weapon that makes
the Lord of Death stay away from one's family and lineage.

वेद शास्त्र और पुरान श्रुतियों के वचन, एक सार है नारायण नाम जपन ॥
हरि बिना जप तप धरम करम के उपाय, नहीं आवश्यक व्यर्थ ये श्रम सब जाय ॥
वह हरिपाठ से गहन शांति में खोये, कली फूल रस मगन मधुकर होये ॥
ज्ञानदेव का शस्त्र मंत्र हरिनाम, यम दूर रहें, कुल गोत्र जिये अभिराम ॥

21

काळ वेळ नाम उच्चारितां नाहीं । दोन्ही पक्ष पाहीं उद्धरती ॥१॥
रामकृष्ण नाम सर्व दोषां हरण । जडजीवां तारण हरि एक ॥२॥
हरिनाम सार जिव्हा या नामाची । उपमा त्या दैवाची कोण वानी ॥३॥
ज्ञानदेवा सांग झाला हरिपाठ । पूर्वजां वैकुंठ-मार्ग सोपा ॥४॥

*kāḷa veḷa nāma uccāritāṅ nāhīṅ, donhī pakṣa pāhīṅ uddharatī.*
*rāmakṛṣṇa nāma sarva doṣāṅ haraṇa, jaḍa-jīvāṅ tāraṇa hari eka.*
*harināma sāra jivhā yā nāmācī, upamā tyā daivācī koṇa vānī.*
*jñānadevā sāṅga jhālā haripāṭha, pūrvajāṅ vaikuṅṭha-mārga sopā.*

In uttering the Name, there are no restrictions of duration and time.
Know that the families of both parents are saved.
The name Rāma Kṛṣṇa removes all faults;
Hari alone is the savior of dull-witted individuals.
Who can describe incomparable fortune of a person whose tongue is dedicated to the name of Hari, which is the essence of all scriptures?
For Jñānadev, the *Haripāṭha* is so complete that the path
to Vaikuṇṭha (the abode of Viṣṇu) is made easy for ancestors.

उच्चार हरिनाम करे काल सीमापार, जानो दोनों पक्षों का हो जाये उद्धार ॥
राम कृष्ण नाम से सब दोषों का निस्तार, जड जीवों का हरि ही है तारनहार ॥
हो गयी जीभ जिस की शास्त्र सार हरिनाम की, उपमा कौन बताये उस के भाग्य की ॥
ज्ञानदेव कहें परिपूर्ण हरिपाठ जो अपनाये, आसानी से पूर्वज भी वैकुंठ जा पाये ॥

22

नित्यनेम नामीं ते प्राणी दुर्लभ । लक्ष्मीवल्लभ तयांजवळी ॥१॥
नारायण हरि नारायण हरि । भुक्ति मुक्ति चारी घरीं त्यांच्या ॥२॥
हरिविणें जन्म नरकचि पैं जाणा । यमाचा पाहुणा प्राणि होय ॥३॥
ज्ञानदेव पुसे निवृत्तिसी चाड । गगनाहुनि वाड नाम आहे ॥४॥

*nitya-nema nāmīṅ te prāṇī durlabha, lakṣmī-vallabha tayāṅjavaḷī.*
*nārāyaṇa hari nārāyaṇa hari, bhukti mukti cārī gharīṅ tyāṅcyā.*
*hariviṇeṅ janma narakaci paiṅ jāṇā, yamācā pāhuṇā prāṇi hoya.*
*jñanadeva puse nivṛttisī cāḍa, gaganāhuni vāḍa nāma āhe.*

Those beings are rare who repeat the Name incessantly.
The Lord of Lakṣmi is close to them.
Bhukti (fulfillment) and four-fold mukti (liberation)[9] reside in
the homes of those who repeat "Nārāyaṇa Hari Nārāyaṇa Hari."
Know that without Hari, life is hell itself.
That individual is the guest of the Lord of Death.
When Jñānadev asked what Nivṛtti thought,
he said, "The Name is wider than the sky."

नित्य नियम नाम का करे जो, ऐसे प्राणी हैं दुर्लभ, साथ सदा हीं उन के रहते लक्ष्मी के वल्लभ ॥
रमे जो नित्य 'नारायण हरि नारायण हरि' नाम में, भुक्ति और चारों मुक्ति बसे उन के धाम में ॥
बिना हरि के जन्म नरक समान, प्राणि बना है यम का मेहमान ॥
ज्ञानदेव ने पूछा निवृत्ति का विचार, बोले, नाम का गगन से ज्यादा विस्तार ॥

[9] See footnote 4.

23

सात पांच तीन दशकांचा मेळा । एक तत्त्वीं कळा दावी हरि ॥१॥
तैसे नव्हे नाम सर्व मार्गां वरिष्ठ । तेथें कांहीं कष्ट न लागती ॥२॥
अजपा जपणें उलट प्राणाचा । तेथेंहि मनाचा निर्धारु असे ॥३॥
ज्ञानदेवा जिणें नामेंवीण व्यर्थ । रामकृष्णीं पंथ क्रमीयेला ॥४॥

*sāta pāñca tīna daśakāñcā meḷā, eka tattvīṅ kaḷā dāvī hari.*
*taise navhe nāma sarva mārgāṅ variṣṭha, tetheṅ kāṅhīṅ kaṣṭa na lāgatī.*
*ajapā japaṇeṅ ulaṭa prāṇācā, tetheṅhi manācā nirdhāru ase.*
*jñanadevā jiṇeṅ nāmeṅ-vīṇa vyartha, rāma-kṛṣṇīṅ pantha kramīyelā.*

The universe consists of seven, five, three, or ten or altogether twenty-five principles.[10] The Lord shows that this is only a play of one principle: the supreme Self. (It is very hard to study this.)
But the path of repeating the Name is the greatest of all paths.
There are no efforts necessary.
The repetition of ajapā-japa or "So'ham" mantra that goes on with the breath is also natural. But one needs to go beyond even this; the prāṇa needs to turn in the opposite direction (i.e., the kuṇḍalini must be awakened). To do this takes the firm resolve of the mind.
(But in the repetition of the Name, no effort is necessary.)
For Jñānadev, life without repeating the name is futile.
He has taken up the path of repeating "Rāma Kṛṣṇa."

मेला बनाये तत्त्व सात पांच तीन दस, एक तत्त्व हरि दिखाये कला सरस॥
वैसा नहीं नाम, सब मार्गों में है वरिष्ठ, इधर समझने में होते नही कष्ट ॥
अजपा जप में, प्राण का उल्टा प्रवाह, मन को निर्धारित करने से ही राह ॥
नामबिना व्यर्थ ज्ञानदेव का जीवन, रामकृष्ण पथ का ही किया है वरण ॥

[9] The seven are the five elements (space, air, fire, water, earth) plus prakṛti (nature) and puruṣa (individual soul); the five are the five elements; the three are prakṛti, individual soul, and Self; the ten are the five senses of perception plus the five senses of action; the twenty-five are nature, the individual soul, mahat-tattva (Lord), ego, the five elements, the ten senses, mind, and the five tanmātras.

24

जप तप कर्म क्रिया नेम धर्म । सर्वांघटीं राम भाव शुद्ध ॥१॥
न सोडी रे भावो टाकी रे संदेहो । रामकृष्णीं टाहो नित्य फोडी ॥२॥
जात वित्त गोत कुळ शीळ मात । भजे कां त्वरित भावनायुक्त ॥३॥
ज्ञानदेवा ध्यानीं रामकृष्ण मनीं । तेणें वैकुंठभुवनी घर केले ॥४॥

*japa tapa karma-kriyā nema dharma, sarvāṅ-ghaṭīṅ rāma bhāva śuddha.*
*na soḍī re bhāva ṭākī re saṅdeho, rāma-kṛṣṇīṅ ṭāho nitya phoḍī.*
*jāta vitta gota kuḷa śīḷa māta, bhaje kāṅ tvarita bhāvanāyukta.*
*jñānadevā dhyānīṅ rāma-kṛṣṇa manīṅ, teṇeṅ vaikuṅṭha-bhuvanī ghara kele.*

While performing japa, penance, rituals, practices, and righteousness, have the feeling that in every being there is Rāma.
(That also is the culmination of the spiritual practices.)
Never leave this feeling. Abandon all doubts.
Always hail Rāma Kṛṣṇa with great fervor.
Transcend caste, wealth, creed, family, and character and start singing the praises of the Lord right away, full of devotion.
Jñānadev's meditation and mind are Rāma Kṛṣṇa. Hence, the world he lives in has become Vaikuṇṭha, the abode of Viṣṇu.

जप तप क्रिया नियम और धर्म थाम, घट घट में रखो शुद्ध भाव राम ॥
भाव मत छोडो, जा हो संदेह पार, नित्य रामकृष्ण की हो जोर से पुकार ॥
पार कर गोत्र-शील-जात-कुल धन, क्यूं न करे शीघ्र भावसंग तू भजन ॥
रामकृष्ण ध्यान हुवा ज्ञानदेव मन, बन गया सारा जग वैकुंठ सदन ॥

25

जाणीव नेणीव भगवंतीं नाहीं । हरिउच्चारणीं पाही मोक्ष सदा ॥१॥
नारायण हरि उच्चार नामाचा । तेथें कळिकाळाचा रिघ नाहीं ॥२॥
तेथील प्रमाण नेणवें वेदांसी । ते जीवजंतुंसी केवी कळे ॥३॥
ज्ञानदेवा फळ नारायण पाठ । सर्वत्र वैकुंठ केलें असे ॥४॥

*jāṇīva neṇīva bhagavantīṅ nāhīṅ, hari-uccāraṇīṅ pāhī mokṣa sadā.*
*nārāyaṇa hari uccāra nāmācā, tetheṅ kaḷi-kāḷācā righa nāhīṅ.*
*tethīla pramāṇa neṇaveṅ vedāṅsī, te jīva-jantuṅsī kevī kaḷe.*
*jñānadevā phaḷa nārāyaṇa pāṭha, sarvatra vaikuṇṭha keleṅ ase.*

In the Lord, neither knowledge nor ignorance exist
(since He is all knowledge.)
Repeating the Name always leads to liberation.
Where the name "Nārāyaṇa, Hari" is uttered,
the age of Kali has no access.
Even the *Vedas* cannot fathom the importance of repeating the Name,
how can an insignificant individual being understand?
For Jñānadev, the fruit of repeating the name "Nārāyaṇa" is that
the whole universe has become Vaikuṇṭha, the abode of Viṣṇu.

ज्ञान या अज्ञान भगवान में नहीं, मोक्ष है सदा हरि उच्चारण में ही ॥
जहाँ होत नारायण हरि नाम का उच्चार, वहाँ कलि काल को नहीं प्रवेश द्वार ॥
वेदों में भी नाम महिमा पूरी नहीं आई, फिर जीव समझे कैसे उसकी क्या बढाई ॥
फल पाया ज्ञानदेव ने ले नारायण नाम, हर जगह हो गयी वैकुंठ विष्णुधाम॥

26

एक तत्त्व नाम दृढ धरी मना । हरिसी करुणा येइल तुझी ॥१॥
तें नाम सोपे रे राम कृष्ण गोविंद । वाचेसी सद्गद जपे आधी ॥२॥
नामापरते तत्त्व नाही रे अन्यथा । वायां आणिक पंथा जाशील झणी ॥३॥
ज्ञानदेवा मौन जपमाळ अंतरी । धरोनि श्रीहरी जपे सदा ॥४॥

*eka tattva nāma dṛḍha dharī manā, harisī karuṇā yeila tujhī.*
*teṅ nāma sope re rāma kṛṣṇa goviṅda, vācesī sadgada jape ādhī.*
*nāmā-parate tattva nāhī re anyathā, vāyāṅ āṇika paṅthā jāśīla jhaṇī.*
*jñānadevā mouna japamāḷa aṅtarī, dharonī śrīharī jape sadā.*

The Name is one principle; hold it firmly in mind.
Hari will have compassion on you.
That name is easy: Rāma Kṛṣṇa Govinda.
Sing it in a voice choked with emotion.
There is no principle other than the Name.
Don't waste your time switching quickly between different paths.
For Jñānadev, it is the Lord who repeats the Name,
holding the silent jāpāmālā within.
(By that, Jñānadev means that the breath that goes on incessantly
is the jāpāmālā; the Lord holds and repeats the Name silently.)

एक तत्त्व नाम दृढ मन में धर, आयेगी हरि को करुणा तुझपर॥
सुलभ है रे, बोल राम कृष्ण गोविंद कह ले, भावविह्वल वाणी से जप तो पहले ॥
नाम सिवा नहीं तत्त्व कोई और, जल्द बदल पंथ करे क्यूं और दौड ॥
ज्ञानदेव मौन जप माला भीतर, स्वयं श्रीहरि जपते निरंतर ॥

27

सर्व सुख गोडी साही शास्त्रें निवडी । रिकामा अर्धघडी राहूं नको ॥१॥
लटिका व्यवहार सर्व हा संसार । वायां येरझार हरिवीण ॥२॥
नाममंत्र जप कोटी जाईल पाप । रामकृष्णीं संकल्प धरुनि राहे ॥३॥
निजवृत्ति काढी सर्वमाया तोडी । इंद्रियां सवडी लपूं नको ॥४॥
तीर्थवर्ती भाव धरी रे करुणा । शांति दया पाहुणा हरि करी ॥५॥
ज्ञानदेवा प्रमाण निवृत्तिदेवीं ज्ञान । समाधि संजीवन हरिपाठ ॥६॥

*sarva sukha goḍī sāhī śāstreṅ nivaḍī, rikāmā ardhaghaḍī rahūṅ nako.*
*laṭikā vyavahāra sarva hā saṁsāra, vāyāṅ yera-jhāra hari-vīṇa.*
*nāma-mantra japa koṭi jāila pāpa, rāma-kṛṣṇīṅ saṅkalpa dharuni rāhe.*
*nija-vṛtti kāḍhī sarva-māyā toḍī, iṅdriyāṅ savaḍī lapūṅ nako.*
*tīrtha-vratīṅ bhāva dharī re karuṇā, śāṅti dayā pāhuṇā hari karī.*
*jñānadevā pramāṇa nivṛtti-devīṅ jñāna, samādhi sañjīvana haripāṭha.*

It (the Name) is the sweetness of total bliss.
All six scriptures have concluded this.
Even for half a moment, do not remain idle, without repeating it.
All the meaningless transactions of this world lead one
through the useless cycle of birth and death.
Repeating the mantra of the Name, millions of sins drop away.
Hold onto the thought of Rāma Kṛṣṇa.
Extricate all your tendencies, cut off all attachments;
don't hide behind the senses.
Have faith in the holy places and rituals and always have tenderness,
peace, and compassion. With this, make Hari your guest.
Jñānadev has direct knowledge given by Lord Nivṛtti
that the Haripāṭha brings life-restoring samādhi.

मधुरता सब सुखों की छहों शास्त्र के मन भाये, आधी घडी भी आलस्य में मत गँवाये ॥
झूटा व्यवहार यह सब संसार, हरि बिना आना जाना है निस्सार ॥
कोटी पाप जायेंगे नाम मंत्र जप, राम कृष्ण का दृढ धर संकल्प ॥
निज वृत्ति निकालो, सारी माया तोडो, इंद्रियों के पीछे छूपना छोडो ॥
तीर्थस्थान और व्रत में भाव धरो, करुणा-शांति-दया से हरी को पाहुना करो ॥
निवृत्तिदेव के ज्ञान से, ज्ञानदेव प्रमाण पाया, हरिपाठ समाधि संजीवन लाया ॥

28

अभंग हरिपाठ असती अठ्ठावीस । रचिले विश्वासें ज्ञानदेवें ॥१॥
नित्य पाठ करी इंद्रायणीतीरीं । होय अधिकारी सर्वथा तो ॥२॥
असावें एकाग्र स्वस्थचित्त मन । उल्हासेंकरूनी स्मरण दीवीं ॥३॥
अंतकाळीं तैसा संकटाचे वेळीं । हरि तया सांभाळी अंतर्बाह्य ॥४॥
संतसज्जनानी घेतली प्रचीति । आळशी मंदमति केवीं तरे ॥५॥
श्रीगुरु निवृत्ति वचन प्रेमळ । तोषला तात्काळ ज्ञानदेव ॥६॥

*abhaṅga haripāṭha asatī aṭṭhāvīsa, racile viśvāseṅ jñānadeveṅ.*
*nitya pāṭha karī iṅdrāyaṇī-tīriṅ, hoya adhikārī sarvathā to.*
*asāveṅ ekāgra svastha-citta mana, ulhāseṅ karūnī smaraṇa dīviṅ.*
*aṅta-kāḷīṅ taisā saṅkaṭāce veḷīṅ, hari tayā sāṁbhāḷī aṅtarbāhya.*
*saṅta-sajjanānī ghetalī pracīti, āḷaśī maṅdamati keviṅ tare.*
*śrī guru nivṛtti vacana premaḷa, toṣalā tātkāḷa jñānadeva.*

The *Haripāṭha* consists of twenty-eight abhaṅgs.
Jñānadev has composed them with conviction.
Whoever always reads this on the banks of Indrāyaṇī[11]
becomes powerful in all respects.
Make the mind remain one-pointed, at peace,
remembering the divine cheerfully.
At the time of death as well as calamity,
Hari protects that person within and without.
The saints and good people have verified this for themselves.
How can a lazy, dull-witted person go across?
By Śri Guru Nivṛtti's loving words, Jñānadev is delighted instantly.

हैं हरिपाठ के अट्ठाइस अभंग, रचे ज्ञानदेव ने विश्वास के संग ॥
इंद्रायणी के तट पर नित्य पाठ कर, आ जाता अधिकार सब पर ॥
हो जाये एकाग्र स्वस्थचित्त मन, कर के उल्लास से दिव्य सुमिरन ॥
चाहे संकट हो अंतिम काल, भीतर बाहर उस का हरि लेते सम्भाल ॥
संत सज्जनों ने तो पाया है अनुभूति सार, मंदमति और आलसी कैसे होवें पार॥
श्रीगुरु निवृत्ति के वचन प्रेममय, ज्ञानदेव को हुवा संतोष उसी समय॥

---

[9] The name of the river on the banks of which Alandi is situated.

जय जय विठोबा रखुमाइ...
*jay jay viṭhobā rakhumāi...*
Hail hail to Viṭhobā Rakhumāi...

Finale
अखंड जयां तुझी प्रीति । मज दे तयांचि संगति ।
मग मी कमळापति । तुज बा नाणीं कंटाळा ॥१॥
पडून राहिन तये ठायीं । उगाच संतांचिये पायीं ।
न मागें न करीं कांहीं । तुझी आण गा विठोबा ॥२॥
तुम्ही आम्ही पीडों जेणें । दोन्हीं वारती एकानें ।
बैसलों धरणें । हाका देत दाराशीं ॥३॥
तुका म्हणे या या बोला । चित्त द्यावें बा विठ्ठला ।
आतां न पाहिजे केला । अवघा माझा अव्हेर ॥४॥

*akhaṅḍa jayāṅ tujhī prīti, maja de tayāṅci saṅgati.*
*maga mī kamaḷāpati, tuja bā nāṇīṅ kaṅṭāḷā.*
*paḍūna rāhina taye ṭhāyīṅ, ugāca saṅtāṅciye pāyīṅ*
*na māgeṅ na karīṅ kāṅhīṅ, tujhī āṇa gā viṭhobā.*
*tumhī āmhī piḍoṅ jeṇeṅ, donhīṅ vārati ekāneṅ,*
*baisaloṅ dharaṇeṅ, hākā deta dārāśīṅ.*
*tukā mhaṇe yā yā bolā, citta dhāveṅ bā viṭṭhalā.*
*ātāṅ na pāhije kelā, avaghā mājhā avhera.*

Those who have incessant love for you, give me their company.
Then, O husband of Lakṣmī, I will not bother (bore) you.
I will just lie down in that place quietly, at the feet of the saints.
I won't ask you to do or say anything, I swear this to you, Viṭhobā.
Our bothering of each other will go away with this one thing.
I have sat at your door pleading to you.
Tukā says, "O Viṭṭhala! Please listen to these words.
Now, please do not forsake me, in whatever manner."

अखंड जिन्हें तेरी प्रीति, मुझे दो उन की संगति ।
ऐसा हो कमलापति तभी, मुझ से आप उब न जायें कभी ॥
पड रहूँ उसी स्थल में, ऐसे ही संतों के पाद तल में ।
कोई और न माँग लाऊँ , विठोबा! आप की सौगंध खाऊँ॥

तेरे मेरे बीच की तनातनी, दोनों इस एक बात से मिटनी ।
बैठा धरना दे तेरे द्वार, कर रहा हूँ यही पुकार ॥
तुका कहे इस अर्जी पर, ध्यान देना विठ्ठल! कृपा कर ।
ऐसा करना चाहिये अब तुझको, किसी तरह ना ठुकराना मुझको ॥

**ज्ञानेश्वर माउली, ज्ञानराज माउली तुकाराम ।**
*jñāneśvara māulī, jñānarāj māulī tukārām ...*

# CREDITS

Umesh and Chitra Nagarkatte

Umesh and Chitra Nagarkatte met Swami Muktānanda Paramahansa (Muktānanda Baba) in 1972, who showed them how to taste the sweetness of the saints' poetry and experience its sublime, uplifting quality. Jnaneshwar was a favorite saint of Muktānanda Baba and in 1974, in one of the visions he bestowed on Chitra, she saw young Jnaneshwar writing the *Jñāneśvari*. Chitra passed away due to complications of a tear in the ascending aorta on August 14, 2018. In the ambulance to the hospital, a chant of Hari's name, "Kṛṣṇa Govinda, Govinda Gopālā," was spontaneously coming out of her mouth.

Dana Wilkinson

Dana Wilkinson spent many years in the divine influence of Baba Muktānanda, from whom he caught the love of the Maharashtrian poet-saints, such as Jñāneśvar and Tukārām Maharaj. Singing Jñāneśvar's *Haripāṭha* has become the heart of his daily spiritual practice.

# SHANTI MANDIR

SHANTI MANDIR, a spiritual nonprofit organization, is dedicated to the propagation of Baba Muktānanda's teachings. One of the ashrams of Shanti Mandir is near the banks of the River Ganges, at Kankhal, near Haridwar. The ashram at Magod is in rural surroundings, amidst a twenty-acre mango orchard, in the state of Gujarat. The third ashram in India is adjacent to the samādhi shrine of Bhagavān Nityānanda, in the village of Ganeshpuri, in Maharashtra state. Shanti Mandir's ashram in the United States is on 294 wooded acres outside the town of Walden, New York. Under the guidance of Swami Nityānanda, Shanti Mandir symbolizes peace, progress, and love. In addition to the spiritual practices carried on daily, these ashrams contribute their resources toward the following charitable activities: Śrī Muktānanda Sanskrit Mahāvidyālaya (education), Shanti Arogya Mandir (health), and Shanti Hastkala (economic upliftment through handicrafts).

Bhagavān Nityānanda

Baba Muktānanda

Mahāmandaleśvara Swami Nityānanda is from a lineage of traditional spiritual teachers in India. While carrying the traditional teachings, he makes spirituality a practical part of modern daily reality, guided by the prayer "May all beings live in peace and contentment." Born in Mumbai, India, in 1962, Swami Nityānanda was raised from birth in an environment of yoga and meditation. His parents were devotees of the famous ascetic avadhūta Bhagavān Nityānanda, and then became disciples of his successor, the renowned Guru Baba Muktānanda. Swami Nityānanda was trained from childhood by Baba Muktānanda and initiated into the mysterious path of the Siddha Gurus. He learned the various yogic practices, including meditation and Sanskrit chanting, and studied the philosophies of Vedānta and Kashmir Shaivism. He was initiated into the Sarasvatī order of monks in 1980 at eighteen years of age and was given the name Swami Nityānanda by Baba Muktānanda. In 1981, Baba Muktānanda declared Swami Nityānanda would succeed him to carry on the lineage. In 1987, Swami Nityānanda founded Shanti Mandir as a vehicle for continuing his Guru's work and subsequently established four ashrams. In 1995, at the age of thirty-two, at a traditional ceremony in Haridwar, India, the ācāryas and saints of the Daśnām tradition installed him as a Mahāmandaleśvara of the Mahānirvāṇi Akhārā. He was the youngest recipient since the inception of this order. Currently Swami Nityānanda, also known as Gurudev, travels around the world, sharing the spiritual practices in which he has been trained.

Mahāmandaleśvara Swami Nityānanda

LOKĀḤ SAMASTĀḤ SUKHINO BHAVANTU

MAY ALL BEINGS BE CONTENT

www.ingramcontent.com/pod-product-compliance
Lightning Source LLC
Chambersburg PA
CBHW071223070526
44584CB00019B/3134
* 9 7 8 1 7 3 2 1 4 2 0 7 7 *